Inherent Resolve

An African American Teacher's Dilemma

By

August Summers

In the Beginning

It was only my third day and I had already been late twice. The walk from the subway station on the Grand Concourse passed Yankee Station and up the hill to Community Elementary School 73X was a good fifteen minute walk and I knew my kids were already lining up in the schoolyard waiting for me.

It was my first year teaching and New York's Board of Education placed me in a small community elementary school in the Bronx which I didn't mind. It was a two hour commute from Jersey where I now lived but I loved the idea of being able to affect young lives. I had this sense of giving back which I must have inherited from my father who'd also stated his illustrious teaching career in the Bronx. I loved the idea that I was not just teaching but had the opportunity to teach little Black and Puerto Rican boys and girls, many of whom had been written off a long time prior to my arrival on the scene.

I was in good physical shape but that hill took everything I had and so I stopped at the corner bodega midway up and grabbed a regular coffee and a buttered roll. A throng of young toughs hung outside and I nodded as I made my way through their small posse. I knew they were checking me out as much as I was checking them out but somehow we remained at an impasse. I'm sure they were wondering who the newcomer to their block was and if I posed a threat to their business enterprises. Little did they know that even though I wore the social worker's suit jacket and tie I posed no threat. They wanted no problems and neither did I and still I knew there were questions.

I had no time to worry about their perceptions now though I was late.

Mr. Linwood Cooper, my principal, stood in the schoolyard at the head of my class. Nervously I assumed my position at the head of my class and watched my fourth grader's faces as they broke into their happy faces.

Mr. Cooper never said a word concerning my tardiness and I wondered if he had me on some probationary period and was simply being patient enough to let me hang myself. Being a stern man I never considered the fact that he may have had some compassion and said or realized that I commuted two and a half hours each way, each day and was at the mercy of both the Jersey and New York mass transit authorities. No, he was not that compassionate. He'd spent too many years in the classroom refining that stern, unwavering teacher face that had suddenly taken on a life of its own and become fixated to his whole being. There were no equals. There was nothing but students of which I was one and after a stern look he finished his morning announcements and walked back into the red brick building. I led my class to our classroom and allowed them to get settled.

Exuberant I challenged them to ask themselves the tough questions each and every day. What was the best and worst thing about your day, your home, your block?

For most of my kids life didn't afford them a moment to stop, think and exhale. Their young lives consisted of simply surviving. The things I now took for granted like where my next meal was coming from were very real concerns to them and they fought with every bit of their hearts and souls to make do not ever stopping to ask why they were in this situation while the rest of the world seemed to march to the beat of a different drummer.

It was quickly brought to my attention that I was purveying my values and attitudes upon my children and 'why should they be expected to think of things outside of their reality?' It was a good question and an undue amount of guilt fell upon me but I let the questions remain. Perhaps they hadn't considered why they thought the way they thought, and fought the way they fought but I was young and naïve and believed in a holistic approach to teaching. I saw these children for the most part as pure and untainted by a society that for the most part had already thrown them away and locked them into generational poverty.

But because they had been and knew of nothing else was no reason I couldn't at least challenge them to think and ask themselves why certain conditions existed. Once they understood why they had been locked in then we could proceed with the next question. How can I extricate myself from what appears to be my destiny?

I once heard, world famous jazz trumpeter Branford Marsalis refer to children and their critical thinking patterns. 'Children don't think. They react.' His observation seemed so profound and yet I'd never considered this. But because they hadn't been able to think in the past did that mean they were destined to make the same mistakes their parents made. Not if I had a hand in the making. I looked at my students as my children all with their own beautifully unique personalities. They all had been blessed with certain distinctive qualities that made them stand out and apart from and in contrast to each other. I saw it as my job, my responsibility, my gift not as a member of the underclass but as a parent and a family member to illicit the best in helping them to reach their full potential.

The boys that stood on the streets outside the bodega had not been given the opportunity to see and dream. They had not been shown anything aside from the Bronx streets so full of crime and drugs and violence. They were not given the opportunity to realize that there was something aside from this and so they plied their trade knowing that they would eventually do some time in Rikers until graduation when they would be promoted and sent upstate to some federal prison for some more serious crime.

It was all a part of the game and they accepted it because there had been no other alternatives or avenues out of the ghetto. I knew and I understood because I had grown up less than twenty minutes from there in Queens and the same narrow avenue was available to me.

The only difference between myself and them was that I had parents who brought me up in the same crime infested streets yet showed me that there was so much to be had in addition to the mean streets of New York. They aroused my interest in reading at a very young age and allowed me to dream and travel vicariously. They exposed me to things and ideas that I could only dream about. They whet my appetite, invoked my curiosity and caused me to search and broaden my horizon and let me know that the world lay at my feet for the taking. There were no stop signs, no pumping the brakes. If I could see it then I could be it. That was the way in which I was raised.

By the time I graduated high school I was intent on exploring the world so I joined the Marines with the hopes that I would travel and see the world and to some extent I did but it did little in terms of challenging my mind. I needed more so on my return home I immediately enrolled in college and completed that in a little more than three years.

I wasn't absolutely sure what I wanted to be at that point in my life but I knew that college was a place I could quench my thirst for knowledge and my father was a strong proponent of one pursuing education for the sake of educating oneself. And I can remember him quoting John Dewey on several occasions.

"Education is not preparation for life; education is life itself."

My father believed that knowledge had its own intrinsic value and a liberal arts degree at the undergraduate level would serve me well in helping to create a broader knowledge base and horizon. I came to embrace a wide spectrum of interests during this time and the inquisitiveness would serve me well. My knowledge base which included a very practical critical thinking contingent enabled me to sidestep many a pitfall as I traversed life's trials and tribulations. And it was this concept that I believed to be essential in my children's surviving the genocide taking place in our urban areas.

It was funny though. I counted the opportunity to teach and impact the lives of these little brown boys and girls as a blessing from God the Father and after paying my rent you wouldn't have known I'd gotten paid. I bought little or nothing. I wanted nothing other than to teach my children. I was obsessed and they drove me. I'd opened Pandora's Box.

It was now close to Thanksgiving now and I had complete control of my class. They prided themselves on being Mr. Brown's students and that meant being the best. They had to. I couldn't and wouldn't allow them to be anything but the best. Not only were they a reflection of me but they owed it to themselves to realize their potential and I pushed them to the very brink and believed that if they reached for greatness and failed then they could settle for excellence. I believed that and I made them believe that. My God had blessed me with twenty four wonderful children and allowed me to have an opportunity to somehow shape their lives to the best of my ability.

I guess I was somewhat naïve but I can remember going home to see my father who doubled as my mentor and complaining that here it was Thanksgiving and I still hadn't received textbooks for my children at which time my father suggested that I look at the glass as being half full instead of looking it as half empty. Confused I stared a blank look covering my face.

'Textbooks are confining. Not only are they confining they force you to work with someone else's curriculum. Without a curriculum to hinder you you have the freedom to write your own. You know your student's and their needs. Now you can develop a curriculum without cultural bias that best suits the needs of your children.

There's a plethora of handouts and other materials surrounding Black history in my study. Feel free to use them. I pored over boxes and boxes of materials designed by my father and his colleagues for teaching inner city kids and soon had a composite sketch of what it was I wanted to teach my children and which direction I wanted to take them.

One of the fondest memories I had as a child growing up in Queens were the Saturday afternoons I spent with my father. During these outings my father and I would take the bus to Jamaica Avenue and visit one of my father's friends. My father's friend was the owner of a wonderful little bookstore and I was given the liberty to browse and choose any items that I promised to read.

My father used to tell me wonderful stories of African American heroes like Frederick Douglass, Nat Turner and John Brown just to name a few and in the aqaWbackground I'd listen to the daily discussions surrounding the Civil Rights Movement which both my parents were very active in. The 'movement' as it was known to me played out in on the nightly news and in my own backyard and brought forth a whole new set of heroes that included Martin Luther King Jr., Malcolm X and Huey P. Newton. These men were my equivalent of Sir Lancelot and the Knights of the Round Table and served as my own real live superheroes.

After whetting my appetite and telling me bits and pieces about the glory, spirit and courage of these men I had to wait 'til Saturday to find more information concerning these men. And the more I read of the great African city of Timbuktu and Hannibal's conquests the more proud and enamored I became of Africa and the plight of African Americans who had suffered so many indignities at the hands of our captors.

The strong foundation built from my readings and my father's teaching instilled in me the pride so sorely needed in establishing a strong groundwork in which to build my life. What made me come to realize how important this foundation was one day standing before my class and preparing for our Thanksgiving program when I suggested that Thanksgiving celebrated the Pilgrims surviving their first year in the New World. I followed the brief history of the Pilgrims so commonly recited in school with the naïve question as to how Blacks or better yet African Americans get here. I thought the key word African in African American would be a sure giveaway but these same children who only moments before had thrown their hands up when I asked about the Pilgrims had no clue as to how their own ancestors had arrived here. When I mentioned that we originated from Africa and had been captured by Europeans and brought here as slaves I received a reaction that I never expected.

'I ain't no African.' And I ain't runnin' round no jungle with bones in my nose', they laughed and joked. I have to admit I was more than a little surprised of their concept of Africa and Africans. To them, (eighty percent of which were of African descent), Africa was not just the Dark Continent but the home of cannibals and animals and in no way were they to be linked with this uncivilized land or its people. I looked out the window of my class and saw Yankee Stadium and remembered a day or two earlier asking them to identify Yankee Stadium which was only a five minute walk from their neighborhood. When no one could correctly identify the house that Ruth built with all of its reputation and history I knew that I had my work cut out for me. And now this.

I immediately realized that until my children had a solid foundation rooted in pride in themselves and their heritage it would be hard to build the self-belief and self-confidence needed to prosper and thrive in spite of the overwhelming odds already stacked against them and so I began here. Someone once said that a house built upon sand can never stand. I believed this.

In the coming weeks I took my father's approach and designated any spare time to telling them the same stories my father told me. And they too were caught up in the rapture as I told them stories of the great king of Mali Mansa Keita still known to this day as the richest man who ever lived. I told them of his haj to Mecca and how his caravan included 60,000 men, including 12,000 slaves who each carried four pounds of gold bars and heralds dressed in silks who bore gold staffs, organized horses, and handled bags. Musa provided all necessities for the procession, feeding the entire company of men and animals.

Those animals included 80 camels which each carried between 50 and 300 pounds of gold dust. Musa gave the gold to the poor he met along his route. Musa not only gave to the cities he passed on the way to Mecca, including Cairo and Medina, but also traded gold for souvenirs. It was reported that he built a mosque each and every Friday.

Musa's journey was documented by several eyewitnesses along his route, who were in awe of his wealth and extensive procession, and records exist in a variety of sources, including journals, oral accounts, and histories. Musa is known to have visited the Mamluk sultan of Egypt, Al-Nasir Muhammad, in July of 1324.[17]

But Musa's generous actions inadvertently devastated the economy of the regions through which he passed. In the cities of Cairo, Medina, and Mecca, the sudden influx of gold devalued the metal for the next decade. Prices on goods and wares greatly inflated. To rectify the gold market, Musa borrowed all the gold he could carry from money-lenders in Cairo, at high interest. This is the only time recorded in history that one man directly controlled the price of gold in the Mediterranean.[18]

In 2014, because of Musa's control of gold and other resources in his lifetime, Musa's wealth was calculated to be $400 billion dollars (in 2014 dollars),[19] making him the richest human being in recorded history.

In a community where material things tended to mean so much I didn't see this as a bad place to start. They were captivated and now that I had their attention I started fielding their curiosity and feeding them tid bits here and there to spur their interests. And then I sat back and watched as the thirst for knowledge began to take hold and as long as they were eager and chomping at the bit I felt it my duty to bombard them with new ideas and concepts. Often times I could see that I wasn't reaching them and would become frustrated that they weren't showing respect for a subject I had devoted many a night to preparing especially for them. I had long ago come to the realization that too often a meal at a buffet only served as sustenance. Yet, that very same meal adorned with garnish and all the trimmings was much more appealing and so I took careful measure in the presentation which often times made all the difference in the world as to whether the meal at hand was palatable. And still after all the preparation had been done

and my lines rehearsed there were many a day my words fell on deaf ears despite my preparation. It was on these days when my own frustration would set in and I would be at my wits end trying in earnest to get twenty eight individuals to bond in unison. That's when you pause and get a feel for where they are, what's on their minds, what's happening at home and in their lives. They will tell you. The classroom quickly becomes a confessional and if you take the time to listen closely you can hear all that's wrong with the world. If you just listen you will come to know and see their parents through their eyes, know their hopes and fears and dreams. This is a very important process that teachers often overlook.

I remember talking to my father one day after a particular trying day. No matter what subject I tried I couldn't get their interest or attention. As I said it was one of those days. When I first got home I had all I could do to just sit down and unwind. Sitting there I rehashed my performance and for the life of me couldn't understand why on this day I had absolutely no success in garnering their attention. It wasn't the first time this had happened and so I added a wrinkle or two for times such as this. Now each morning when I stopped by the corner bodega I would pick out a bag of nickel candies. Their favorites were Now-N-Later so I might grab a couple of dollars worth and during the course of the day I would walk around my class and drop a pack on one of my students desk for working so diligently or behaving so well.

I'd pay them a compliment. 'I really like the effort you're putting forth Damien', I wold comment handing him a pack and shaking his hand or giving him a hug. He would smile, elated that I had taken particular notice and bear down even harder. The other children who were by now quite aware of Damien's new status and wanting the same star status would reassert themselves to their studies.

When other classes were hard at work in class and we were changing classes I demanded silence in the halls. We were to walk with our heads held high and carry ourselves with dignity in public. This I reinforced with verbal praise and other contingents and we became known as the best behaved class. And each time we would receive praise I would ome back and reinforcement there positive behavior with praise and a small celebration which might simply equate to a little more free time or allowing them to choose an activity of their choice.

I had long ago come to the realization that Piaget's experiments with conditioning dogs was just his means of drawing a correlation between the conditioning of man and animals.

In Piaget's experiment he would ring a bell and the dogs would come and there would be a plate of food awaiting them. After awhile the dogs would begin salivating as soon as they heard the bell. Similarly, when a child is rewarded and given positive reinforcement when he or she behaves in a certain way it only tends to reinforce the positive behavior with the hopes of eliciting a reward. In this way, (I used to refer to it as

'positive manipulation'), behavior is modified and will in turn lead to a more productive classroom and more productive students.

But then there were those days like today that with all the persuasive tactics and strategies that a teacher must arm himself with to allow him to maintain discipline and order in creating a positive learning environment go all the window.

Turning on the mellow sounds of Sade I went over my day and sought out my own deficiencies. Finding more than a few things that I could improve on I called on my father seeking advice. After listening for a few minutes my father stopped me. He was smiling when I saw little to smile about. Perhaps he didn't understand. Funny thing was he did understand. After more than twenty years in the classroom he understood completely.

'Son what you are experiencing is what every teacher experiences from time-to-time no matter how good a teacher they are. There's no remedy or cure in the traditional sense but once you recognize this then you simply forego the lesson plans you had planned for the day. At times like these you may want to put the books and papers away and relax. Your approach was the correct one. Change the focus from teaching to learning. Sit back and listen to your students and find out just what is on their minds that prohibits you from doing your thing. Listen and learn. Often a child has more important things on their minds than math and language arts. Your listening and learning your

children is essential to you being able to meet their needs. If a child has lost a family member even the most interesting accounts of Louis & Clark's westward journey will seem boring and unattractive. At other times, they will sit there mesmerized hanging onto your every word. These times are known as 'maximum or optimum teaching moments' and you must recognize these times and run with it. Today however was not what you might call an optimum teaching moment. It's nothing personal but just something that happens and you just have to chalk it up and let it go.'

I listened to my father and let it go.

In the following weeks, my fears were all but diminished by the enthusiasm my kids exhibited in the classroom. We'd been asked to participate in Thanksgiving program and they were thrilled. One of the greatest joys in life for a child is to perform for his parents and with the Thanksgiving Day program they would be able to do just this.

I guess my own enthusiasm played a large part in theirs. I was so excited, so intent on it being a success and my students attaching another storied success to their resumes that I took on the challenge with the same mindset a playwright takes on his Broadway debut. The program's success began and ended with my children representing themselves well. Since we were in the midst of teaching the dynamics of the African slave trade, (by now they readily accepted that they were descendants of slaves), and how

it differed in doctrine from slavery I had each student take a paragraph from the Declaration of Independence and place it on a index card. This index card they carried everywhere and recited the words whenever they had any excess time on their hands. When they had it memorized we read it over in its entirety and analyzed it.

'So, why if they said 'all men are created equal' did they treat us like slaves?'

The questions they raised gave me hope. No longer did they accept things as they were but they were beginning to think. They were beginning to question. They were beginning to think and that to me is the first step in the process of educating.

I had a few parents who saw the patience, the care, the love and the compassion I showed their children and there was nothing that they wouldn't do for me. So, when I called for volunteers to help with the Thanksgiving program I wasn't at all surprised when the parents came out of the woodwork.

Growing up Black, middle class to educate hard-working parents I too got caught up in the stereotypical portrait depicted by the media when it came to America's poor and minorities. For many Americans this is a convenient way to compartmentalize and understand other ethnic groups without having to do the legwork. And I must admit that I too was a victim of taking this shortcut but my first teaching position in one of the worst ghettoes in the Bronx alleviated all that.

I can remember when Reagan was in the White House and America was in dire economic straits. In his attempts to waylay the growing economic concerns and the ever-increasing unemployment rates Reagan parried the growing concerns by Americans calling Russia the Evil Empire and inventing a Star Wars Program which would shoot Russian nuclear missiles from the sky.

The idea was ludicrous and naming Russia the Evil Empire even more insane. I believe it was the world renown singer 'Sting' who summarily asked 'Does that mean that the Russians don't love their children?' I thought this so profound and had to ask myself based on the same premise. Because a people are born into poverty causing them to live in crime infested drug areas where the options for climbing the corporate ladder are bleak at best does that mean that they don't love their children?

I was to soon find out that I didn't have a parent that wanted to see their children grow up and fall victim to the streets. No. They supported me in every way conceivable so that their children would have the opportunities that they were never afforded. The way they saw it is little Black man offered hope and change and an avenue out of the ghetto and if I asked for some help in showing their children that there were other options then I would have all at I required.

Even the bad boys and thugs that hung out in front of the corner bodegas understood that I brought hope and no longer did they eye me wearily but addressed me with respect when they saw me.

'What's up Mr. Brown? How's Hector doing? He doing his homework? I stays on him about school. He give you any problem you just let me know.'

They were out there every day on the grind. This was the life that they had chosen or because of lack of opportunity the life that had chosen them but they knew at seventeen and eighteen that this was not the life that they wanted for their younger brothers and sisters. And no matter how late or how dark it was when I left to go home I never feared walking those so called mean streets. I was protected because I brought hope for the children.

So, when the Thanksgiving program was announced I had more volunteers than needed. My children and I decided that they would dress up in slave attire which consisted of a pair of britches and a muslin shirt and recite the Declaration of Independence which was a paradox in itself.

I had several mothers design and sew my children's costumes and overall it was a resounding success.

My children were so excited about having their parents attend and asked if I were bringing anyone and I thought this would be a good time to let them see a part of my own

life so I invited my fiancée who showed up looking even better than I could have imagined. They wanted to take part in my life and wanted me and mine to take part and share their lives. When it was over they ran up to her and began showering her with a multitude of questions. Although overwhelmed she handled their questions patiently and thoroughly and they became enamored with the woman that had Mr. Brown's attention.

'Is he mean at home?'

'No. Why do you ask?'

'Cause he's real mean to us.'

'Oh, he is not. You're just spoiled and like him and want all his attention and you think he you're his only student,' Jeanette said in my defense.

'I am not spoiled and you know you like him too. Yu said he was cute.'

'Oh, no you didn't. See that's why I don't tell you nothing. You can't ever keep a secret,' Jeanette said embarrassed that her little secret was out.

And then there was Angela. Angela was a cute, little Puerto Rican girl that all the kids used to pick on. She was sweet and a little slow but I refused to have her tested and stigmatized by the label special education and after conferring with several other teachers I respected, (and I could count them on one hand and have fingers left over), I decided to work with her to the best of my abilities and prayed that I could help her overcome her deficiencies. This wasn't a hard decision because she wanted to learn in the most ardent of ways. And the support system I had arranged for her would not let her fail. That and

the fact that her mother was my most fervent supporter coming dangerously close to crossing boundaries on several occasions we were hell bent on making sure Angela succeeded.

'You're Mr. Brown's girlfriend?' Angela asked.

My fiancée noticing the jealousy and heartbreak in Angela's eyes deferred.

'I wouldn't say that. I'd prefer to say that Mr. Brown and I are just good friends.'

'Oh, good,' she said jumping up and down before running away with a renewed sense of hope.

And there was Damien.

'Hi. My name is Damien.'

'I'm Cecilia. I have heard a lot about you Damien.'

'Uh oh. I'm one of his good students. I don't give him a hard time like those fools,' he said pointing to Hector and Victor who were now racing around the auditorium.

'Yes. Damien is one of my prize students. I told him I'm going to adopt him and take him home with me.'

The chubby little boy broke into a wide grin.

'Do me a favor Damien. Go get Hector and Victor and tell them I want to see them now. No sooner than I said that the boy was gone.

'You know these kids idolize you,' Cecilia said.

'I love them too.' Hector and Victor stood before me now. They were two of my favorites. Both were exceptionally bright and perhaps the worst two I had behaviorally but they knew I loved them dearly and would have gone to the ends of the earth to see that they made it and didn't get caught up in the throes of street life which cast a pale shadow over them.

'Why did I have Damien tell you to come and see me?'

'Cause we were running in the gym,' Hector volunteered.

'And if you know that's not what you were supposed to be doing why is it that I had to call and remind you?'

'I don't know. Maybe it's because we weren't thinking,' Victor volunteered.

'And what happens when you don't think?'

'Bad things happen.'

'And you want bad things happen?'

'No.' they both concluded in unison.

'Then what do we have to start doing?'

'Think before we act.'

'Good but in any case that's not the only reason I wanted you two meet my good friend Ms. Branch.'

Both boys looked at the floor and then each other and began laughing.

'What do you say?'

'Nice to meet you miss.'

'Hector and Victor are two of my brightest students.'

'So, I've heard. I've also heard some other things about Hector and Victor.'

Before she could finish Victor shouted out.

'Don't believe what those other teachers say. They're fuckin' prejudiced. Just ask Mr. Brown. He doesn't have any problems with us. Do yu have any problems with us? It's them ol' prejudiced crackers.'

Cecilia was stunned. Me, on the other hand was used to Victor's outburst.

'Come here Victor,' I said smiling and hugging the skinny little boy who had most of the school in fear of their lives.

'And what happens when we have those outbursts in public Victor.'

'I know. I know Mr. Brown. I'm feeding into the negative stereotype they already have of us.'

'And do we care?'

'No.'

'So why is it so important that we don't curse and lose control?'

'Because we are doing a disservice to the kings and queens that came before us.'

'There you go. So, I can count on you to carry yourself in a more dignified manner and show that you are the descendant of kings and queens?'

'Yes sir. Can I go now?'

'Yes sir. But you never asked why I called you.'

'Yes?'

'I just wanted to tell you that you did a great job on your speech tonight. I am very proud of you.'

Victor did not respond but only blushed deeply before grinning broadly.

'Now go and get your classmates and tell them I want to see them. By the way Victor are your parents here? I'd like to meet them.'

'No sir. My dad had to work and my mom was too busy,' he said walking away.

'That's half the problem right there. I've done everything I can to get his parents involved. He may be my brightest student but he needs a push and from what I gather he has no support system at home.'

'That's a shame.'

'It really is and he bothers me more than all my other students combined. He's the sharpest of all my students and the one closest to the streets. If I lose him I don't know what I'll do.'

Moments later Victor was back but this time it wasn't to see me but to see Cecilia.

'Did Mr. Brown tell you that he invited me over when the weather gets nice?'

'I don't believe that's what I said Victor.'

Victor smiled.

'I said I was going to take my two Students of the Month for the month of May to a Yankee game and home for the weekend.'

'Oh, and you think that'll be you Victor?'

'You already know. It's already a lock. It'll be me and one of the Hector's will be fighting for second runner up. I just hope it ain't no girl who wins. I'd hate to have to share my weekend with some girl. No offense miss.'

My class met with many of their parents in tow and after meeting them I congratulated them on a fabulous performance. They in turn shook my hand and

congratulated me on their children's performances as well as thanking me for having made a difference in their children's lives.

'So you're Mr. Brown,' one mother said reaching to shake my hand. 'I had to come tonight to meet this Mr. Brown. I'm so sick of hearing Mr. Brown said this and Mr. Brown said that,' she said grinning. 'So, I told the twins I was going to get a babysitter tonight and go meet this Mister Brown. You know all jokes aside but this is the first time I've seen my twins come home and without me having to say a word they come home and do their homework and lay their clothes out and in bed without me telling them just so they can get up and go see Mr. Brown.'

'Well, I'm glad to hear that. Bridgette and Jeanette are two of my best behaved students. You have certainly done a job in raising them Ms. Anderson.'

'I can now understand their attraction. You're a handsome little thang. You married Mr. Brown,' she said winking at me.

'I don't have time to be married Ms. Anderson. When you have twenty eight children that need your constant attention it hardly leaves time for a wife,' I said smiling.

It was funny but there was a direct correlation between the parents that showed up and were involved in their children's lives and the progress of their children.

Every now and then the question arises from politicians and educators as to where to place the blame for our failing educational system. Teachers and educators blame the

parents. Parents place the blame on the inability of the schools to educate and the beat goes on. There is no debate and no viable solution and the issue remains dormant until the next election. Meanwhile are children are failing miserably. From my rather limited perspective both teachers and parents are at fault. From what I have seen there are far too many so-called teachers who lack neither the passion nor creativeness to teach. And though there remains a shortage of teachers it is an incredible disservice to place our greatest natural resource in the hands of some who does not have the zeal or fervor needed to elevate our children to greatness.

I said all of that to say that there is a direct correlation between parents who make the painstaking sacrifices to become good attentive parents and the success of the child. I understand that many of us are not capable of being good parents simply because they do not have the knowledge of what it takes to be a good parent. And if you are unaware and entrust the education of your child to an inept teacher who can neither service o address the child's needs then there is a good chance that that child will become a part of the prison industrial complex. Statistics support this.

It is therefore our duty as Christians and Americans to insure that our children are equipped with the tools not only needed to survive but thrive and prosper.

II. Raul

I spent a good deal of the Thanksgiving break trying to come up with some things I thought would inspire my kids and was thrilled when it was over and I was back in front of the class.

'Raul? Raul Martinez? Has anyone seen Raul?'

'I saw him every day during the break,' Hector shouted out.

'Well why isn't he in school?'

Hector began to hedge now. If it was one thing my kids understood at an early age was that you didn't snitch or squeal on people. It was a ghetto law that they all adhered to even at this young an age.

Raul was an enigma. A big boy he'd been left back twice and so he towered over most of my other children but he was amiable and polite. My bad boys used to tease him and run when he did attend school but he would dismiss them good–naturedly and I liked this about him. I'm quite sure the other student's teasing about his size and being left back bothered him but he always took it in stride and when he finally had had enough he would chase them and catch them before threatening but always with a smile and never did he try to hurt the smaller younger children. At best Raul was an average student and there was no reason he should have been left back but his attendance or lack of prevented him from being promoted and the way it was looking now he would be left back again.

There were several days either my children or I would be looking out our third floor classroom window and see Raul either walking to the store at his own leisurely pace or passing by the school on his way somewhere.

He was one of mine and the mere fact that he wasn't attending already meant that he'd narrowed his opportunities to the streets and jail and this to me wasn't an option so I sat down with my principal and then my father both older Black men who had half a century in the New York Public School System and in their wisdom both told me something that I had hard time swallowing.

My principal Mr. Cooper listened. He'd seen it over the years and I do believe earnest and stern in his approach he had some empathy and compassion when listening to me when it came to Raul's truancy. Knowing my passion he urged me not to go to Raul's house for my own safety believing that it was in his best interest to protect the welfare of his teachers even if they did not have enough common sense to protect themselves.

'If things seem slightly ajar already as to why cannot come to school on a regular basis then why you think I would send one of my teachers into that already rather risky and tenuous situation.'

My father was of a similar mind although he had a more holistic and worldly perspective when he said 'you're not going to save them all,'

Neither of my mentors saw my going to Raul's home as a wise choice and I must admit that I had my own apprehensions but I was enamored by the idea that I could save all of my children and being that Raul was one of mine there must be no effort saved in rescuing Raul from the inevitable.

Directly after the final bell rang and I dismissed my class I set out for auel's house with my buddy Mike Martinez the school's security guard in tow.

Raul's family lived less than a half a block from the school. Mike and I walked the three flights up to the apartment and knocked.

'Who is it?'

'It's Raul's teacher Mr. Brown.'

A few minutes later the door opened and two young Puerto Rican gentlemen stood on either side of the room holding guns. A white haired old lady sat on the couch between them. In front of her was a living room table with a mountain of cocaine on it. Waving to the two young men to lower their guns I stood awaiting eye contact with the older woman.

'This is Raul's grandmother. She doesn't speak any English so I'll translate for you.'

I didn't have time to be in shock when it came to the guns and drugs although I was.

'Yes mam. I am Raul's teacher and the reason that I stopped by is because of Raul's attendance. He's a bright kid and he needs to be in school if he's to have a fighting chance out here in this world.'

Looking down at the floor I thought I saw a slight grin as her grandson translated. She then looked straight at me and began in broken English which her grandson translated.

'You are right about Raul. He is a bright boy and he's a good boy. And all he talks about is Mr. Brown. I think he likes you as well as you like him. I will see that he gets to school,' she said. 'Thank you for coming to see me about Raul.'

That had gone well despite me thinking otherwise when I saw the guns and the drugs. Still, I do believe that when your heart and soul are in the right place and you walk with God that no harm can befall you. And yet I was glad that whole affair was over.

Raul never did come to school on a regular basis although after going to visit his grandmother I did see him three or four times that week. After that it was back to his old pattern and then I did not see him at all. I used to wonder what happened to him but if anyone knew that he wasn't attending school it was his his family and grandmother and if they condoned or had him running on their behalf then in the name of self-preservation I

needed to steer clear of whatever it was that was keeping Raul away from school. It hurt and I suspected he was being groomed for the drug trade and there was little I could do.

III. The Closing of the School Year

The months rolled by and I could see the overall progress of my class. It was nice to see the enthusiasm they now had for learning and I had little to do now other than to whet their appetites and they were off to the races absorbing everything that came their way. By the time spring came along everyone was on board and excelling being my wildest expectations and they clamored for more.

Months before I'd promised that when the weather broke I'd take two of my students to a Yankee game and home with me for the weekend. When the week came and we had come up with the judges and the criteria for Student-of-the-Week they were chomping at the bit. I can honestly say that there was little difference in their behavior since they were well behaved most days but the diligence they put into their class work, homework and participation was far beyond their usual efforts.

Each day of the week they would surpass the day before and when the week was over I let my two assistants decide as to who was the Student-of-the-Week as I was so proud of them all I would have taken them all home.

When the voting was all over it was as Victor had predicted and it was he and Hector who won. They both had had exceptional weeks and it only reaffirmed my faith in the beliefs that teachers could make a difference and that given the proper stimuli children even from what we believe to be the worst economic conditions can achieve the highest heights.

I loved my bad boys. I loved them because they were bright and energetic and mischievous. They had spirit and wouldn't back down if they felt they were wronged and it didn't take much to set them off. I loved them because they were typical New York City kids and I felt the vibe.

It was just a shame that we had several faculty members who didn't get them. What I saw as beautiful they despised. I can remember one middle aged bleach blonde from Yonkers who had finally gotten out of the classroom and away from these little Black and Puerto Rican children she so despised. The only reason she was here in the Bronx was because it was so close to Yonkers.

Now she had a cushy job in the library next to my classroom and was so bored that she would pop out to talk to me anytime she heard my door open. She had a penchant for Victor who happened to be my favorite and would as apropos of catching a glance at Victor who was always teasing someone or making some outlandish comment

that would have both his classmates and his teacher laughing uncontrollably. That was just Victor and why all that met him and truly got to know him loved him so. And despite a horrid home life he somehow found a way of making those around him laugh.

'Mr. Brown have you read Victor's files?'

I wanted t say no. Victor is not an inmate with homicidal tendencies. Victor is a child like any other child with needs and desires. It is our job to supply Victor with the fulfillment of his needs so that he can grow and mature into a productive human being. We must meet him where he is and guide and prod and cajole him into achieving as much as possible in the short amount f time with him. That should be our goal with Victor. That's what I wanted to tell her and perhaps what I should have told her. But I knew even at that young an age, (I believe I was twenty-eight), that there was no changing the attitudes of many of my co-workers who believed that working with these children was like doing some type of penance for some wrongdoing they had committed in their lives.

On another occasion she came into my classroom after a small but very vocal celebration to see what was wrong. My kids were ecstatic about a recent announcement I'd made and were literally bouncing off the wall when she walked in. Walking over to me she looked at me before commenting.

'Look at them. They're just like a bunch of little chimpanzees.'

There was no need for me to say anything. I'd grown up in this New York. I had long ago grown accustomed to this. I believe it was my father who once told me that the government could legislate civil rights but they couldn't legislate attitude. There reasons for their being there were varied but the fact that none of their reasons had anything at all to do with serving our children did not bother me in the least. I had long ago ceased to allow the negative energy of others in any way influence my spirit and in most cases chose to avoid those of this persuasion. They found fault in the way Mr. Cooper ran the administrative part of the school. They did not like the Black and Puerto Rican children who attended our school. They did not like the parents or the community and yet we handed our children over to these s0called caretakers to give our children guidance, caring, love and compassion while providing the necessary tools to become a viable member of our society.

When I brought this up at the dinner table one night both of my parents became engaged and told me of similar instances in their lives.

My mother summed it up best.

'You just keep teaching those children and don't worry about the naysayers. Remember they talked about Jesus.'

Not wanting to give it too much thought I nevertheless thought about about the words to The Serenity Prayer.

> God, grant me the serenity to accept the things I cannot change,
> The courage to change the things I can,
> And the wisdom to know the difference.

I adhered to this with little difficulty and I readily accepted the fact that I could not erase the hatred and bigotry that so consumed far too many of my co-workers but what was even harder for me t accept was how any adult could come to hate a child.

My children were not immune to this deliberate and unashamed behavior and although only ten and eleven years old they readily recognized the racism directed towards them and had already had a defensive and combative stance when confronted.

I understood and supported them in attempts to deal with it but at the same time I warned them about focusing on the negative.

'Life is too short to focus on ignorance. There comes a time in a person's life when there is nothing you can do. And at that point it can become lethal and there is no reasoning with it. All that you can do when confronted with it is to understand that it is an illness that you can only sympathize with as you walk away before you too become infected.' In other words, turn the other cheek. Still, and as we have always done we dismissed it and continued to progress in spite of.

I'd promised and one thing I came to realize about children over the years is that they put an undue amount of trust in you when they do come to take you into their

confidence. So, if you say you're going to do something you must follow through and honor your word or you may lose the child's faith and respect.

Even so I hated the thought of taking Jose and Victor home with me for the weekend. The effort I put forth during the week to assure that my kids had everything and would want for nothing was exhausting at best. The daily commute from Queens to the Bronx was two and a half hours each way and that alone was exhausting. And I usually spent my weekends just laying around trying to recover and then preparing for the upcoming week. Now there would be no break, no time to recharge.

I promised my boys a trip to a Yankee game and so after taking them downtown to dinner we headed home and after inspecting the house and talking for awhile they were both asleep and I figured this might not be too bad after all. The following morning my ideas for a quiet and uneventful weekend came to a screeching halt. At first I thought I was dreaming when I heard the knocking at my bedroom door. I then remembered my boys and glanced at the clock before turning to the cool side of the pillow and going back to sleep. I was then awakened for the second time that morning. Seems Victor and Jose had found their way to the backyard and climbed up to my window and jimmied it open. I opened my eyes to their smiling faces poking through my bedroom window wanting me to get up and wondering what was on the breakfast menu.

I took them down to the local park after breakfast to play basketball. I ended up the only one shooting around. They seemed more than content to fire away at me fom the bleachers asking me every question conceivable in getting to know their teacher and what made him tick.

Following the park I arranged a small barbecue before the Yankee game and invited a friend over. Hector and Victor were tickled with all the fuss I made over them and I only hoped they would be too tired to attend the game. I hated making the two and a half hour commute when I didn't have to but there was no denying them.

Now this was the mid-nineteen eighties and big cassette boxes were all the rage to the new and emerging hip hop culture in New York City at this time. The bigger the box the bigger the sound and I guess it was sort of a type of prestige you garnered if you had a really big box. I for one bought into this and had one of the biggest boxes around. When Victor and Hector saw this I had new credence and they took turns carrying it and letting the music blare.

We took the subway up to the Bronx and Yankee Stadium that evening and of course Hector had to carry the box which was almost as big as he was. Yankee Stadium was packed and I knew and warned him that he would have problems carrying the box in the crowd but Hector insisted and soon found himself being jostled about. At about this

time a man of say about forty didn't notice the young lad with the monstrosity attached to his shoulder. Not looking below the man accidentally bumped into Hector who went off on a tirade like none I've ever heard before. When he'd finished he'd threatened the man and all his offspring. I initially thought the man was going to go medieval and behead my charge but he was good-natured and reserved and smiled as much in shock as I was at the array of profanities that came from the youngster's mouth while I apologized and scooped him up, box and all and whisked him away.

I'm not sure either the boys or I knew who won the game but we had a ball. We arrived home well after midnight. I think we were all dog-tired and there were no questions or conversations that night. Sunday brought an end to the weekend and even though the boys had a blast they too were ready to get back home.

At school Monday morning Hector and Victor recounted the events of the weekend to their classmates adding a touch here and there to insure the jealousy of their classmates. So, prolific were their tales of grandeur and splendor that the rest of my children began that day competing to see who would be the next Student-of-the-Week and assuring me at different times during the week that they would be the next winner. What they didn't know was that as much as I enjoyed Victor and Hector it would be some time before I volunteered to take my children home with me again.

The rest of the school year went fairly well and the praise for my efforts in my first year of teaching were unprecedented. And to top that off my class came in second in

overall progress within a year's time. I was truly proud of this accomplishment but two things hurt me deeply and overshadowed even this.

The first was that after all my efforts my brightest student, Victor hadn't passed and was the only one of my students to be left back. Even Raul had aged out and was being promoted. I don't know if Victor or I was more hurt over this latest revelation but I was devastated and no matter what I said in his defense it all fell on deaf ears. It seems he had failed the end of grade test and that was it.

Of course, I had to run this whole charade by my father who always somehow had a way of putting things into perspectives.

'You have to understand that teaching and dealing with the lives of other human beings is and can never be an exact science. There are simply too many variables involved. And with that said remember that even the greatest teacher cannot serve the world. In other words as intently and earnestly as you try you will not be able to either reach or save all the children.'

I knew he was right and understood but it didn't mean that Victor's or my failing hurt any less.

The final blow came on the last day of school at dismissal when I sent my children home for the very last time. They were all smiles and laughter as they had been since I met them nine months before. It was after all, the last day of school and the first day of summer vacation. They jumped and laughed and hugged me. They had worked

hard and been promoted and now they were free. Meanwhile they stood and watched the tears flow from my eyes. It was time to turn the page. This chapter was over. And I only hoped that I had somehow changed their lives and inspired them to hope and dream and to aspire for greatness.

The Blessed Teacher

I went on to work for the Bureau of Child Support after teaching as a caseworker for the city and was responsible for sending Black and Puerto Rican men to court for not paying child support. The job itself was quite simple. Perhaps the easiest way to send these men to court was to send them a certified letter to their home and their last place of employment. A signature from either home or work was an omission of where they were and where a warrant could be served. Once the warrant was issued then they had to be in court to face the charges and made to pay child support. Call it the way I was raised but the fact that a man had a child meant that that man was responsible for the welfare of that child. There were no shortcuts and o way around it.

My grandfather had ten children; five boys and five girls, migrated from Mississippi to southwestern Pennsylvania where he worked in the coal mines for the next fifty or so years bought himself a thirteen acre farm and raised his children with little or no education. Four of my five uncles, his sons were married with children and they followed in his stead. They were all hard workers and all of them took care of their children and were good fathers. I think they prided themselves on that mere fact and nothing else. To them manhood meant taking a wife and raising and providing for your children.

I came to the Bureau of Child Support with these same ethics and beliefs. I had no conception of why a man would neglect to take care of his child. But there were other factors which I had hardly considered up until this point.

Was the brother surviving? What type of work did he do and could he afford to take a third of his check and pay child support? Would he be able to survive after paying child support?

Years later after my son Christopher was born and I had taken custody of him when his mother and I separated. She was living in North Carolina and I'd picked up and moved to Charleston South Carolina. I believe Chris was six at the time and from time-to-time he would look at me with those big, brown eyes of his and ask me when we were going to see mommy. I was working three jobs at the time. One was to pay bills and maintain the household. The second covered my car payment and the third was simply to pay for his child care which was close to two hundred dollars a week. When I told people what child care cost me I was told that two hundred dollars was relatively cheap. It may have been but I rarely had a dollar left over.

In any case, I would pack a bag and make the call telling Cecilia that I was on my way. I do believe we still loved each other despite our differences and two months after this trip I was told that Cecilia was pregnant again. Nine months later I received the call.

'Bert. You have a beautiful baby girl.'

I grabbed Chris and made the three hour trek in two hours receiving two speeding citations along the way. I was elated with my beautiful, brown little girl and knowing that a child had a better chance of making it and becoming a more wholesome individual with two loving parents I thought a reconciliation was in order. Since I had to be at work the following morning and Chris had school our trip was abbreviated.

We returned home that evening. The next day as I returned home from work I picked up the mail and found a letter from the South Carolina Bureau of Child Support requiring that I pay three hundred and six dollars a month in child support for my newborn daughter. Now I understand how bureaucracy works and how often times we remain nameless and our individuality is disposed of but the fact remained that I had two children and no one was lending any type of financial aid, (and I certainly could have used some help), but the fact that bothered me so was how the state could demand that I pay when I already had my son. It just seemed to me that if there were two children by two parents and I had one then Cecilia, the mother of the two should take one if I had already assumed responsibility for the other one. I don't know if I was correct in my thinking but there just seemed to be some fairness to my way of thinking. Yet, the state never asked and I knew in my present condition that I could never pay three hundred dollars a month in child support. So, the next day I rode back to North Carolina and

packed up my daughter and brought her to live with me. With three low paying jobs I could never have paid what they were asking.

Still, it was the principle that drove me more than anything. The phobia of being considered a dead-beat dad that didn't take care of his children would have been something hard for my personality type to have digested. But that didn't stop me from having compassion for the absent parents I was responsible for sending before the judge. After interviewing hundreds I understood their plight and empathized with the majority.

'I'm a pizza delivery man Mr. Brown. I take home a hundred and eighty five dollars a week working full time. I stay at home with my moms and my younger brothers and sisters because I can't afford to move out. Do you know what real estate is like in New York and I'm just talkin' Brooklyn. Oh, my God! Then I try to help out moms and there's nothing left. I mean it ain't like I don't love my daughter. I see her almost every day of the week but I can't afford to take care of her. I'm barely taking care of myself. You know what I'm saying? And now they want to hit me with close to four hundred a month in child support.'

The state didn't take time to understand but I did and using my discretion and common sense I was unable to locate this absent parent and refer him to court. The system was imperfect.

'Do you have receipts for the utilities, and the rent?'

'No. Everything is in my baby's mother's name.'

'Then I cannot declare you head of household Mr. Jacobs. This 39th Circuit Court of Kings County remands you to the county clerk's office where you can devise a payment plan.

I eventually saw it as another way young minority men were lured into the industrial prison complex and wanted no part of it.

Not long afterwards I decided to follow my parents lead and relocate to North Carolina which had an urban flair like New York but didn't move at breakneck speed or made me feel like I was on crack on a Sunday morning.

The truth is I wanted to teach and they told me all that was right with North Carolina and they seemed to love it and I loved them so. A month or so later I relocated and my mother soon had me house hunting. She had it all figured probably even before I arrived. Her son the teacher would move here and change lives, buy a modest home and be close to her. Well, she talked me into almost everything except the home. It was simply too close to her and I valued my privacy.

I was soon back in the classroom though in some rural town five or ten miles outside of Fayetteville in a little town called Raeford with its two sources of employment. One was the turkey plant where ninety percent of my children's parents worked and the only other employment was cropping tobacco. I didn't think it was possible to be any further away from the Bronx and urban life but here I was.

There were two middle schools that fed into the larger high school and I had the rare opportunity of teaching at West Hoke Middle School. My principal was an older white gentleman who walked the halls with his pipe and pot belly that suggested one too many meals. His tie always looked like it was choking the breath from his red, paunchy face. It was hard for me to figure this man at first but then he was the one that welcomed me an suggested that a strong Black man was what he sorely needed to teach those that the other teachers had abandoned for one reason or another. All I could think of was Victor. And I knew there was no way I was going to fail this time. I gladly took the position but middle was a different challenge and there were no teachers to welcome me or suggest that I read any of my children's files.

When the classroom doors closed they went to war. The school was racially split down the middle with fifty percent being Lumbee Indian, (a very interesting story in itself), and fifty percent being African American. The teachers were similarly split with half being white and the remainder being Black. There were no Lumbee Indian teachers.

There were a few white teachers that had long ago grasped the definition of teaching and were thorough and proficient. Then we had the Black teachers much like myself that looked at the teaching of little Black boys and girls as a blessing from God and thought each of their children a blessing and they had but one function in life and that was the elevation of these children to wherever the next level was for that particular child. I would like t think I fell into this category. These I'd like to refer to as those passionately dedicated to the upliftment of our society. And there were those that had no idea of why they were there but they soon found out that they were in over their heads.

I was assigned to the Special Education Department and was given what was being referred to at the time as a self-contained class. This was a class that was not permitted to change class or interact with the rest of the school. My children were labeled children with emotional and behavioral problems. That's how they were labeled but then I have never been too fond of labeling children. A label is like a self-fulfilling prophecy and if anything is content with throwing away or methodically disposing of the children we do not want to deal with.

I can remember going to a Catholic elementary school and the nuns having their hands full with me. I was bright and an only child. My parents doted on me andeducated me at home and school for me meant a means of reinforcing some of the things they taught me and socialization since I was an only child and had limited socialization when

it came to playing with other children. I took this to mean that I was expected to have fun with the other children at school and did my best to comply. My mother was back and forth so much that I do think that was one of the reasons she decided to volunteer. It definitely was a gas saver. She now took me to school in the morning and we would ride home together. But when the nuns pulled her aside to talk about me my behavior was never a concern.

'He's a very bright little boy Mrs. Brown.'

'How's his behavior?'

'He's a bit talkative but then they all are at this age. I attribute that to his being bright.'

'I know how my son can be sister. Let me know if he gives you any problems.'

'Believe me Mrs. Brown when a six year old becomes too much for me to handle it's time I change professions.'

One of the differences between the nuns who taught me and the public schools I've encountered along the way was that the nuns who taught me more-or-less volunteered their time. They received a small stipend but I wouldn't go so far as to call it

a salary. Still, they endeavored going far and beyond the call of duty to teach us. Theirs was a labor of love.

Contrary to that was the teacher who taught my son. My son was also bright and loquacious as was his father and I too had grown familiar with running back and forth to his school when it came to his behavior. On one particular day his third grade teacher suggested I have him tested and give him Ritalin. Now the average parent may have run right out and had his or her child tested and medicated as is the current trend but not I. I recognized him as being bright and she as someone who probably shouldn't have been allowed in the classroom. But in every stigma, label, and stereotype there tends to be some inkling of truth so I took what she'd said along with some of my own observations and studied hyperactivity deficit disorder and decided to change his diet and pray that maturity slowed him to a degree where he could function in a classroom setting.

The results are as follows. At the age of twelve or thirteen I enrolled him into an all-Black charter school called Imani where they stressed African American history and culture and never was I called concerning his behavior. I'm not saying that he had an epiphany and was suddenly transcended into one of Saint Peter's angels. What I am saying is that he prospered in the right setting and with strong family support that was engaged in his education and maturity. Here at Imani with strong Black men and women as teachers who not only understood him but were familiar with little Black boys he was

not deemed a disciplinary problem but a bright young boy. Here it was never suggested that he was disruptive or that he be medicated so he could function within a classroom setting. This is the remedy for teachers who are not avowed to teaching. How much easier is it to have a child take a pill, medicate him then label him as having some sort of learning disability and write him off than to come to know that child and teach him.

My son continued on to high school where and although I saw little in the way of effort on his part he went on to graduate in the top ten percent of his class and received a four year academic scholarship to attend the University of North Carolina. He has long since graduated and I wonder about all the other bright little Black boys who will and have been written off in a similar fashion by some inept white teacher who thinks it beneath themselves to come to know the children he or she is supposed to educate and give guidance to.

I don't know if it's a fair statement to say teachers cared more then or that parochial are as a whole better than public schools but it certainly appeared so.

So, when Mr. Langdon proposed that I take this class of so-called problem children I jumped at the opportunity. He was honest and up front with me when he made his proposal.

'Mr. Brown I want you to think long and hard about accepting the position. Understand what I am proposing. These are the kids that no other teacher wants in his or her classroom. They are all behavioral problems and some are even in the court systems.

Weezus, for example, has been accused with sexual assault by a little white eighth grader. I don't know if he did it or he didn't but I don't want the two to have any contact with her while in school.

Scotty Sturdivant is a little Indian boy who doesn't present any threat but his teachers say he's high all of the time and doesn't do anything but draw. They say he's a pretty good artist but he refuses to do any type of school work.

Davika is another one of yours. I know him, coached him on the football team and he's a pretty good kid and student and one hell of a football player but he's having a hard time. His parents just recently divorced and he hasn't been the same since. He's a good kid though.

Jeremy has no interest in school. His father's a brick mason. He did the front walk to the school. Jeremy worked by his side the whole time and can lay brick as well as any man. He shouldn't be here. All kids weren't meant to go to school.

Then you have Leroi who's not a bad kid but he's a big kid. He may be fourteen or fifteen. Leroi's problem is that he has too many other things going on in his life to allow him to attend school. In the beginning of the school year you may see him once or twice a week but once tobacco season starts you won't see him at all. But Leroi won't pose you any real problems.

And then there's Brett. What I'd like to see where Brett's concerned is half days. Mornings preferably. Brett cannot make it a full day. He's just not capable. I don't know what's wrong there. His older brother who's in the eighth grade is an honor roll student and class president but Brett is for lack of a better word 'crazy'. He's as close to nuts as anyone I've ever seen. If it were up to me I wouldn't allow him to step foot in the door but the school board would have me swinging from the nearest tree if I ever said that. What they fail to realize is that I'm responsible for the safety and welfare of every child in my school and Brett poses a threat to them every time he steps foot in here. I just have to have written proof to substantiate this. What they don't understand is that every one of the people that work hands on with Brett view him in much the same way I do. But you don't really have to worry about him. He attends school even less frequently that LeRoi. There are more but those are your more severe cases.

Like I said think about it long and hard and see if this is something you might want to do. And know this I will not make allowances for any of your students or you. They will be held accountable just as any other student would be should there be an

infraction of the rules. You have my number. Call me if you have any questions.' Mr. Langdon said shaking my hand and rushing off to deal with another matter.

Riding home I thought about the position. It was a challenge but what was life without challenges? I welcomed them. I was right at home in the midst of Black boys considered at-risk or having behavioral problems. What scared me was Mr. Langdon and his cavalier attitude and thoughts.

'All children aren't meant to go to school.'

This was radical thinking to me who always believed that every child should be afforded the right to expand their horizons through education. Of course I believed there were many means to procure an education and I can remember my younger sister being awarded a trip to Spain and the principal of her school remarking to my parents that a trip to Spain during the school year was not in her best interest. My father was livid stating that this trip would do more to enlighten and broaden his daughter's scope of the world than sitting in a classroom for the next two weeks. Needless to say my sister went to Spain and that trip may have done more than any other single event in her life to shape her dreams and desires as to what she wanted to do with her life. She is now in the foreign services and has seen much of the world in her twenty years with the government. And although Mr. Langdon may have been right about every child not being meant to

attend school I still believe to this day that every child should have the opportunity to pursue an education and it is not our right to deny them the opportunity.

A week or so later I called Mr. Langdon to accept the position although I still had my reservations. Despite my reservations about Mr. Langdon I believed that if there was any hope for these youngsters I could very well be their last best chance for them to erase the negative labels that had already been attached to them.

When I walked in the first day I could see they were already apprehensive. Who was this new guy? Was he just another Black man who had bought a suit and tie and continuing with the same old meaningless rhetoric that saw them as criminals and thugs? Or by chance did he bring something different? I could see the curiosity behind their hardened stares.

But unlike my first teaching experience I took the time and glanced their files not to prejudge but to familiarize myself with their names and faces. There was nothing that meant more to a child than to be recognized as individuals. I started off in typical fashion.

'Good morning. My name is Mr. Brown. And it looks like you're stuck with me for the duration of the year so let's lay down some ground rules and maybe you can help me and just maybe and if you allow me I may be able to help you. This is a self-

contained class which means that you have been assigned to me and are not to interact with the rest of the students here at West Hoke. From what I am told you are the students whose behavior will now allow you to be in a regular classroom. Now I don't know what made them come up with this designation and I don't care. What I am here to do is to make this the best damn class at West Hoke despite the talk.'

'Ahh Mr. Brown you just don't know how it is here. These crackers will write you up if you sneeze.'

'You know Weezus I believe there's a lot of truth in what you say.'

The boy was shocked that I knew his name and smiled broadly glad to know that his reputation preceded him.

"I grew p in Queens, New York and encountered the same things growing up but come on Weezus. You and I both now by now that racism exists and the enemy is you. But after we recognize this fact then what do we do? I'm not here to tell you that racism doesn't exist. I'm here to show you how to circumvent it and all that comes along with it. Racism is perhaps the primary reason we are shot and killed and imprisoned but there is a way of beating it and going ahead and leading successful lives for us and our offspring. What I'm going to teach you is how we go about beating it but I need you to listen and learn.'

A hand shot up. I had their attention now.

'If you follow my instructions we can change their attitudes about us. My goal is not to have them accept us but to be the best class and the best students in the entire school. When we walk down the halls I want them to say 'is that LeRoi.'

LeRoi's head popped up. With the same surprised look that Weezus had he stared at me wondering how I knew his name. I stared directly into his eyes.

'I want the same for you Jeremy,' I said now looking at Jeremy. 'And the same for you Davika. And you too Margaret.' I made eye contact with each of them and they beamed knowing this Black man may somehow be different than the teachers they had previously had to endure.

'The first thing we have to do is learn who we are, where we come from and be proud of who we are as people. We can't let them define us and pigeonhole us and stick us in classrooms where we are isolated and stigmatized as 'bad' children with behavioral problems. That's not who we are. We are the sons of queens and kings and when we walk these halls from this day forth I want anyone who looks at us to know we are different, that we are strong, that we are disciplined and that we won't tolerate any stuff. We can laugh and joke and cut up within our classroom but when we walk the halls we must carry our heads high and be the faces that everyone looks up to. Is there anyone who can't fight? LeRoi is there anyone in this school who can beat you?'

'No sir,' he said grinning sheepishly.

'And I'm sure if I ask the rest of you that then you'll all give me the same answer so here's my question to you. If there's no one in this school who can beat you what's the point in fighting?'

They all looked at me with perplexity.

'There is an old saying that you must choose your battles and fighting and getting into skirmishes is a waste of time. And what's the end result? The end result is you get suspended and get labeled as a problem child. Are you problems? Do you think I look at you as problem children?'

They shook their heads.

'No. I don't look at you as problems because you are not problems in my eyes. I look at you as bright black boys. Sorry Margaret. But they look at you as problems and want to get rid of you. This class is only the first step in their getting rid of you but we're not only going to change their perception but we're going to put you on the path to becoming strong Black men. All I need for you to do is to have faith in me and I guarantee this will be the best year you have ever had in school. Are you willing to take a chance?'

They all nodded yes even though they didn't know me. I knew it was the best offer they'd had. It was an opportunity they had not been given up until this point.

'Are there any questions? Scotty?'

The small little Lumbee boy so hard at work at his desk suddenly looked up when he heard his name called. His eyes were glazed over and I knew he was high.

'Yes sir.'

'Do you have any questions Scotty?'

'No sir.'

I moved to his side and peered over his shoulder to see what it was that he was working on so diligently. I was surprised to find a pretty good caricature of me.

'You're quite talented. Perhaps you can do a mural of everyone in the class and we can cover the far wall.'

'Really,' Scotty said beaming with pride.

'Yes sir. Just let me get permission from Mr. Langdon.'

'Oh, that's the end of that. He ain't gonna let you do it.'

'Let me worry about that Weezus.'

The First Week

The first wee k brought several surprises. I knew I was slowly making headway into my kid's hearts. I'd gotten permission for Scotty to paint the mural and this alone sold him on his new teacher. Every morning he would come to class early and begin working on the mural. Scotty was a man of few words and I didn't force him to say anymore than he was willing to say. He seemed content with the arrangement and I knew that he would open up when he was ready so I stayed out of his way and let him work as long as he kept up with his class work which he now took as seriously as he did the mural he was working on. The boy was unmistakably talented and although I knew little about art I complimented him continuously which seemed to elate him and he toiled throughout the coming days on both his schoolwork and the mural.

In the meantime I took my time trying to get to know my students. Weezus was rambunctious but proved to be very bright picking up concepts as quickly as I threw them out and it wasn't long before I realized that he was far in advance of the rest of the class and grew bored easily. What he needed was to be constantly challenged before boredom set in and he became restless. I had no contingency plan as of yet but I knew that if I didn't come up with one soon I would lose him.

Until I could come up with one I kept him by my side to make sure that he didn't stray and get in trouble. On the third or fourth day, I saw him as I was pulling out of the school parking lot.

'Which way you going Mr. Brown?'

'Home Weezus.'

'Can you drop me off?'

'Get in,' I said opening the car door knowing that this was against school policy.

'Where do you live?'

'Not far.'

Weezus directed me pointing out the different landmarks in Raeford.

'That's Tammy's house,' he said pointing to what appeared a one room wooden log house, The windows were wooden with no screens and a wooden slat that simply turned locked them. I'd read about rural poverty and how the Indians had been dispossessed but I never expected anything like this. There homes were tantamount to the slave quarters I'd visited in and around Charleston, South Carolina years before.

Tammy was a cute little sixth grader with a lot of mouth and a knack for stirring up trouble.

'Most of the Indian kids live here and in the next trailer park.'

'Where does Scotty live?'

'I'm not sure.'

'What can you tell me about Scotty Weezus?'

'Not much. He's cooler than a fan. He smokes a lot but he doesn't bother nobody. His brother and father sell weed but that's about all I know.'

I didn't say anything.

'So, tell me about you Weezus. Do you live close by?'

'Not far.'

'And who do you live with?'

'I live with mother and my grandparents.'

'And where's your father?'

'He lives about three doors down. But he has a girlfriend and two kids by another woman.'

'Does he come to see you often?'

'No. Never.'

'Never?'

'No,' he said dropping his head dejectedly and making me sorry I'd even asked.

His eyes lit up when he saw his house and the old woman tending her flowers in the front yard.

'Come on Mr. Brown. I want you to meet my grandmother.'

I was dead tired, exhausted but I managed to get out ad meet the woman and was glad I did.

'Ma'am Weezus asked me for a ride home.'

'Oh you must be Mr. Brown. Weezus thinks the world of you. Go inside and change your clothes Weezy. I'm so glad that you're here for him. He needs a strong man in his life. His grandfather and I try hard but you know we're getting old and I'm afraid we can't give him all he needs.'

'He mentioned that his father lives a couple of doors down.'

'He don't care nothin' bout the boy. He got himself another woman and has two or three kids by her. He act like he don't know Weezus exists. That's why I'm so glad you're here for him now.'

We went on to talk for another hour or so and I knew that Weezus came from a loving family that only wanted the best for him. She explained the legal problems they were having and after filtering the story from Mr. Langdon, his grandmother and Weezus I came to the conclusion that Weezus was innocent. And still she talked.

I guess we stood there and talked for over an hour about everything from her daughter—Weezus' mother who was mildly retarded to her husband of fifty four years who she loved dearly and owned a plot of land somewhere not far away. She was anxious to find out about me and what made me tick and why I had come to Raeford to teach her grandson.

'Black boys are suffering everywhere. The educational system is a failure in America so Raeford is as good a place to try and make a difference as the next town.'

'Well, we are certainly glad to have you. You know most of the teachers I've met don't give a hoot about Weezus and would just as soon see him go to jail and throw away the key. So, I want to thank you Mr. Brown for taking the time and having his best interest at heart. And if he gives you a hard time you have my permission to take him outside and wear his little behind out. Do you hear me? Weezus knows I don't play and won't tolerate any of his shenanigans.'

'Yes ma'am.'

'And if there's anything you need feel free to call on me or his grandfather anytime.'

'I certainly will and I must say it was very nice talking to you.'

'And to you as well Mr. Brown and if I can remember I'm going to send you a little something for you and your family. Well, that is if I can remember. My minds not as good as it used to be.'

Driving away I thought about the old woman. It was obviously she loved the boy very much and only wanted to see the best where he was concerned. These were simple folks many of whom had never had a college graduate in their family and placed all their hopes on their children and grandchildren to be the first. Not long ago they had been slaves and then sharecroppers and still had close ties with the land.

In any case, I knew Weezus came from a good strong family that loved and believed in him and were receptive and I would be able to count on their support should I need it. It gave me hope and although I knew Weezus would be a challenge but with both teacher and family working in conjunction it would be difficult to fail him. I also realized that the small, young boy commanded the respect of his classmates and if I were to win him over the class would be in tow.

It wasn't hard. Basketball was my favorite sport and any time we had some type of success in the classroom or I felt they had exhibited more than enough effort it was off to the gym. I'd played basketball ever since I can remember and now in my thirties I could hold my own. Weezus though short in stature and slight in build loved basketball almost as much as I did and played any time he could. Did I fail to mention that his grandparents bought him a basketball hoop which stood in the street in front of their house? But by eighth grade Weezus had abandoned the front yard to hang out with the older boys and run with them every chance he got. In no time at all he was holding his own with them.

I remember watching them and being amazed at these middle schoolers who were dunking at six one and six two. Weezus was all of five two and a hundred and ten pounds soaking wet but he could run with the best of them and direct the offense all the while talking more junk than everyone else combined. And it wasn't unusual for one of the older boys to jump into his face and threaten to beat him down if he didn't stop with the trash talk but Weezus would stand toe-to-toe with the bigger, older boys until someone intervened. They all respected him for his basketball skills and heart.

I used basketball in the classroom and after a month or so they knew that if they stayed on task and completed their work in a timely fashion they would be rewarded with some gym time. Over the years I have watched children and often hear my father's words when he would speak of optimum teaching moments and so after I had gotten everything I could possibly get out of them I would release them.

For the most part they were a wonderful class. I didn't have one behavioral problem among them and they rallied around the fact that Mr. Brown loved them and would go far beyond what the curriculum demanded or what was expected. I spent time at their homes, with their families, in their communities and with them after school hours. I made myself apart of their lives and they responded.

There was many a day that I welcomed lunch time. On most days when my one o'clock lunch rolled around I was truly spent. I'd spend the morning acting out whatever it was I was teaching on that particular day and then when I perceived that they had a rather firm grasp of the concept I'd reward them with the gym.

Of course, I was a tad bit older than the kids I was running with. And I felt it every day at lunchtime and would always tell myself that I would not try to run with them tomorrow and then tomorrow would come and I'd be right out there running, sweating and feeling worn-out and exhausted when it was all over.

Lunchtime was my only reprieve. And since I was not like your typical teacher and didn't fit the mold I fell out of favor with many of my co-workers even though I had yet to meet or come to know them. I chose not to eat in the teacher's lounge and this too angered them. I just saw separating myself from my kids as some type of hierarchical misallegiance to my overall goal. I was a bit naïve but I wanted to be accessible to them at all times should they need me.

Many of the other teachers saw this as a little too much bravado and as an attempt to make them look bad which was not my intention at all. At first, when it was lunchtime and my students saw me taking out my lunch and sitting at my desk they too looked me in bewilderment. A couple of days later when I dismissed them for lunch Davika, (who had still not spoken to me and it was now mid November), elected to stay back. My teacher's assistant, Valerie, a rather stately Black woman about my age was insistent on him going but still he refused. I waved her off and let her know that it was alright that he stayed back.

I had been informed by Mr. Langdon that Davika was one of the nicest kids he had and one hell of a football player. But in the past year his parents had divorced and

Davika had gotten into several fights following their divorce and in his last fight he'd totally lost it and put the boy in the hospital. To avoid any further occurrences he'd been placed with me. He hadn't spoken since we'd been together and although I had no problems with him I was curious to know what was on his mind so when he chose to stay with me during lunch I looked at this as a good omen. I'd already called and met with his father who told me basically the same thing that Mr. Langdon had already told me.

'I'm glad you called me in Mr. Brown. Davika's a good boy and he needs someone right through here. I know that he likes you. I overheard him talking to his friends about you. Said you were from New York and were friends with Jay Z and Biggie. Is that true?'

'I'm thinking Davika may have stretched the truth somewhat but to tell you the truth I wish I had more students like him. He does everything I ask of him. The only thing he doesn't do is talk.'

'I know. Like I said he didn't take the divorce well and doesn't trust adults. I think he thinks his mother and I betrayed him. At least that's what the shrink says. Says it's going to take a lot of time and patience to work through this. So, I just give him his time and space and pray a lot. I never meant to hurt him like this. I love my son Mr. Brown.'

The last thing I needed was a parent losing it and I could see that Davika's father was a breath away from breaking down.

'I'm sure everything will be fine and I will be in touch if I see any changes Mr. Johnson.'

The man was huge and now I knew where Davika got his size from. Rising from the desk he grabbed my hand in a firm handshake that buckled my knees.

'Thank you for showing concern for my boy.'

'Your concern is my concern,' I said as we parted company at the front door of the school.

'What was that all about Mr. Brown?'

I turned abruptly only to find Mr. Langdon lighting his pipe.

'It was nothing. I just called Davika's father in to see if he could help me in why Davika refuses to talk.'

'Did he help?'

'Not really.'

Mr. Langdon smiled before relighting his pipe.

'That's like asking the fox what happened to chickens. Mr. Johnson's a good man but when we have a problem with our kids chances are nine times out of ten the problem starts at home,' he commented before walking away.

Now here sat Davika before me mute as usual with seemingly no inclination to speak. And so I went on with my lunch and during that hour not a word passed between us. Whe lunch was over the other kids returned and were surprised to find Davika sitting with me.

'We was wonderin' what happened to you,' Scotty said. Davika never replied but the next day four or five students decided to join Davika and I for lunch. By the end of the week my entire class decided they preferred the classroom to the cafeteria. It made me feel good but soon I had students knocking at my door that I had never seen before. And then during class time I had children knocking at my door telling me that they had been thrown out of there class and asking for my permission to sit in on mine. I would open my door to them if they promised not to disrupt my class. Minutes later they would be out of their seats jumping up and down trying to answer the questions and receive whatever treat I was giving out that day for right answers.

At other times, a teacher from the Special Education department would come knocking at my door livid.

'Mr. Brown would you mind taking Tammy? She refuses to do anything in my class and when I ask her to do anything all she says is she wants to go to Mr. Brown's class.'

I knew Tammy and she could be loud and boisterous but she always had a smile on her face and was as good natured as they come but if she didn't like you she could be a fire starter setting a classroom on fire. Strawberry blonde with blue eyes she was as wild as they come. You say an Indian with blonde hair and blue eyes?

Now the story goes that when the earliest settlers came to North Carolina led by Captain John Smith he left settlers here to form a colony but it seems that there were so many hardships that first winter that their mere survival depended on the local natives. As the story goes the Croatan, (later to be known as the Lumbee Indians), absorbed the settlers into their tribe. When John Smith returned the only evidence of the survivors was the word Croatan carved into a tree. The story goes on to say that this is the reason that the Lumbee is the only tribe to have a trait for blonde hair and blue eyes.

Tammy had all those traits and a fire that burned within her like no one I have ever seen. She was simple and country as they come and it would was nothing for her to jump up on a desk and holler and scream to make her point before hugging me on her way out of the class. I loved her. On those days I was feeling somewhat down and lethargic she would energize me. She ran at full speed constantly and would take nothing less from me or anyone she encountered.

We enjoyed each other's company and now here she was demanding to come to my class. What could I do? I took it as a compliment and aside from her tirades we got along splendidly with her and her behavior was always exemplary.

The problem was it was happening more and more. It was almost as if my class had become a dumping ground where teachers could discard their unwanted. In more instances than not the kids were starting to misbehave so they could come to my class. It was the highest compliment I could receive but it also presented problems.

No longer did I offer rewards. There was no need to. They had gotten it. They weren't in trouble or ostracized for coming to school. And they enjoyed coming to school to see what each new day brought.

We were in quarantine and yet they were happy and I was elated. There did not exist a curriculum for my children. I had one directive from my principal and that was to corral and warehouse these so-called emotionally and behaviorally challenged children with learning disabilities.

But I had no children that fit this category. And accepting them as normal children I found them to be quite bright, receptive and insightful. What they saw as disruptive I quickly turned into the best behaved class in the school. I did not ask or demand anything out of the ordinary aside from them being the best they could possibly be and if they were willing to put forth the time and effort in improving themselves then I would support them in their efforts. I do believe that in time they saw my sincerity and love for them.

I loved them as much as I did my own children and was equally as hard on them. I demanded that they respect me as well as themselves. But most of all I demanded that they respect others regardless of color or the way that they were treated.

I had long ago come to the realization that perhaps the most important subject that they needed to master even before the three 'R's' was critical thinking. Once you could navigate the storm waters with some reasoning and common sense life's dilemmas became but mere speed bumps to slow your forward progress.

Once you set clear goals in place and were steadfast in your plan and had the resolve and were clear in your thinking nothing was impossible. It was essential to their survival for them to think rationally before acting. In cases where they were treated unjustly I implored them to think before reacting. First, look at who it is that is practicing the injustice. Then ask yourself why it is that this person is acting in this manner. If for some reason it is not justified, (and more often than not it is not justified), then why demean yourself because this person has chosen to. As the descendants of queens and kings we cannot diminish

our own value and self worth by confronting this person who has chosen to act in an irrational way.

Then we must look at the repercussions we may suffer by confronting this person. When I was around the same age as my students the Civil Rights Movement had just taken off. Many Black folks, (mostly the older and wiser), took the moderate approach to attaining civil rights and were followers of Dr. King whereas the younger generation of non-thinkers followed Malcolm and the Panthers. All were for the upliftment of Black folks but all three had different tactics or strategies.

Knowing little and simply reacting to the dogs put on peaceful demonstrators; women and children who followed Dr. King caused a knee jerk reaction. Malcolm said that we should protect our women and if anyone puts hands on our women then that person should be killed. And when I saw white racist cops beating women and children with Billy clubs my first reaction was armed resistance. There was no critical thinking. There was just a knee jerk reaction.

But my father always the thinker posed a series of questions that forced me to think.

'So, you believe that Malcolm and the Panthers have the correct response?'

'Yes, I do. Absolutely.'

'And so you think the best way in which to retaliate is to pick up a gun and go to war with these racist cops.'

'Absolutely.'

'Well, let me ask you this. Where will you get the guns?'

'From the store.'

'And who is the largest manufacturer of guns in the world?'

'I dunno. I guess the United States is.'

'So, let me see if I have this right. In retaliation to our women and children being beaten you think arming ourselves and killing whites is the best form of retaliation?'

I nodded affirmatively.

'Okay and with that reasoning let me ask you this. What will you do when you run out of bullets? Will you go to the same man that you are attempting to kill and ask him to give you more bullets so you can attempt to kill him again?'

With age came wisdom but I had not yet matured to the point where I could think. The theory that for every action there is an equal and opposite reaction had never entered my mind. The idea that there was such a thing as repercussions evaded me as well.

There was another aspect that I had not garnered either and that was the fact that there are only certain avenues which can be used in affecting change in lieu of tremendous and insurmountable odds and they must be legal and peaceful to insure your own survival.

These were the messages that I attempted to instill in my children and because they incurred less in the way of trouble they readily accepted this attitude. A 'yes ma'am and yes sir' was a simple way of affecting a positive encounter in the attitudes of others and not only were they able to see a change in the way they were now treated as opposed to the way in which they had grown used to.

I can remember going to stay with my father while he was being treated for prostate cancer at John Hopkins University Medical Center in Baltimore. It was my first time there and I loved everything about it aside from the reason I was there. I enjoyed the feel of the waterfront and the bustling crowds. And I loved the people. They were warm and friendly and I had many an engaging conversation with strangers.

When I told my father this he smiled and said the people appear warm and friendly because that's how you approach them. And now my students were experiencing this very thing.

I would never consider myself an authoritarian. I have far too much of the child left in me to be that. But with love and respect and a genuine and sincere sense of caring you can demand just about anything from a child and they will adhere to whatever it is you demand in hopes of not disappointing you. In the halls I demanded complete silence so my students didn't disrupt the other classes in progress as well as to show the school not only that we had changed but that we were now the best behaved class in the school which we were. At times I would see teacher's staring at my class and whispering.

One day Mr. Langdon called a teacher's meeting after school. I hated these meetings and saw little that was accomplished. I hated being called upon to speak which happened more times than I care to think about but being that they were mandatory I had little choice but to attend. I sat with a first year teacher who I carpooled with off and on. The meeting differed little from the others with five or six teachers' taking the podium to complain about student's behavior and demand Mr. Langdon do something about it. That's when all six foot four of Mr. Langdon rose up. He had had enough.

'You know I sit here and listen to you cry and bellyache about these children. We are all here to teach. So, why don't we focus on that and start teaching for a change. I walk by half of the classrooms and there's a teacher sitting at her desk leafing through some papers or a magazine. I don't know what the class is supposed to be doing but that's not teaching. And then you want to complain about the kid's behavior. If I sat there bored half out of my mind I guess I'd misbehave too.'

He was angry now and he had everyone's attention now including mine.

'At the end of last year I heard these same complaints and we decided to hire a behavioral specialist to deal with our problem children. Funny thing but there aren't a whole lot of folks applying for that position. But I was fortunate enough to find Mr. Brown who took on the challenge and in no more than a month took all your so-called problem children and has the best behaved class in the school. I wish I could make an instructional video of his class for all of you to watch. And I have never yet heard him raise his voice.'

I can honestly tell you this was unexpected and caught me totally off guard. I was embarrassed and only wondered how many more teachers would hate me now? And to this day I have never had a more favorable compliment or one that I hold so highly. I loved to teach and this was the highest compliment that I could receive and it came in front of my peers. There was no place to go but down from here but I refused to let that happen.

It was close to the holidays now and everyone had grown tired of the drudgery that came with school. It was time for a break and I do think both my class and I had grown somewhat weary. I needed some type of motivation to keep my class on-task and motivated. With two weeks to go I came up with all night basketball where my top twenty students that came out on top academically for the two weeks prior to Thanksgiving would be invited to attend. We got out of school the day before

Thanksgiving and from the time we were dismissed until the following morning which was Thanksgiving we'd have a tournament made up of four teams competing against each other until the whistle blew at eight a.m. the next morning.

Most of my boys envisioned themselves the next Michael Jordan so I had no problem with willingly takers and all put forth a great effort during the two weeks prior. My problem was how to eliminate those that had put forth a considerable effort but somehow failed to make the cut.

Mr. Langdon had other fears. He worried about leaving me alone with twenty of what he deemed the worst boys in his school. Yet, when he asked for volunteers among his teachers there was not one taker. I did have help though. Both my teacher's assistants who were both Black, relatively young, (both were in their late twenties), and aware of the plight of our young Black boys and were fully behind my efforts both volunteered their time. I accepted Mr. James. He too was a basketball fanatic and we had talked about starting intramurals if we could find the time. Valeria was my other teacher's assistant and had a good heart and was sincere in her efforts but adamant and very stern and strict. It was obviously she had come from a very good and orderly home where principles and ethics were paramount but where there was no tolerance or patience.

All too often she was the fire starter I did not need. You were going to do because I as an adult told you to do it was her mantra and often times caused more harm than good.. At which time my student's thoughts are, 'and who the hell are *you* coming in here and demanding that I do something? You obviously don't know who you're talking to. You better step the fuck off bitch before you get hurt.'

The day before Thanksgiving we had just such an occurrence with Brett. I don't know if you remember Brett but Brett was the student Mr. Langdon felt he had to fill me in on before I actually met him. Brett is the child that Mr. Langdon did not want in his school. But being that the school board and the state made it a point that every child should be awarded an education Mr. Langdon was forced to open the doors to Brett. And still and all he had gotten them to limit Brett's schooling to half days. In any case, I may have seen Brett three days that whole school year and never really gotten a chance to get to know him. If I'm correct Brett was suspended two of those three days.

Mr. Langdon referred to him as crazy and as that is not my field I cannot tender such a prognosis but what I observed in the two or three days that he was in attendance I would not care to behold again. In any case, for some reason he decided to come the day before the Thanksgiving break and after all the other children had been dismissed Valeria, Brett and I found ourselves alone in the classroom. Brett had someone coming to pick him up and was not allowed to walk around the school without an escort lest someone would end up with a broken nose or arm in the interim. I had no problem and as it was the end of the day before a holiday I felt more relaxed than usual.

I knew my boys were gathering in the gym under Mr. James's supervision and as long as they were focused on playing basketball they were fine. Now all we had t do was wait until someone picked Brett up.

'Have a seat Brett,' Valeria said.

'I'm good,' Brett replied.

'I said have a seat Brett.'

'I don't want to sit. Why don't you leave me the fuck alone? I ain't bothering you.'

'I don't know who you're cursing at. Boy, I'll snatch your lil behind up.'

'Mr. Brown you better tell her something,' Brett said looking at me. But before I could say anything Valeria had jumped up out of her seat in an aggressive stance. I was up from my desk as Valeria blocked the door. On the opposite side of the room stood Brett next to the large pyramid of canned goods my kids had brought in for the less fortunate at Thanksgiving.

'Tell her to move Mr. Brown. My ride is here.'

'You're not going anywhere Brett. I told you to sit your ass down and that's what you're going to do. I don't know what kind of home you come from but where I come from when an adult tells a child to do something they'd best do it. Now sit your ass down before I sit you down.'

Before you could say Jackie Robinson a can of sweet peas whizzed by my ear followed by a can of green beans. He was doing his damndest to hit Valeria but I was in the way. She was ducking one way and I the other. The authorities eventually came and took him away and that is just one of the reasons I declined to have her as a chaperone at our all night basketball tournament. This was a time for the kids to let their hair down, kick back and just have fun and I did not need or want her Gestapo style of discipline in attendance.

I think I ran as much as the kids did playing game after game until three or four o'clock in the morning with our team losing in the finals. Mr. James and I chipped in to purchase a trophy which had engraved on it the 1st Ever All Night Basketball Champions with a player resembling Michael Jordan holding the ball as if he were about to dunk. The kids loved it and we had a little ceremony crowning the champions.

Mr. James and Mr. Langdon chipped in and bought twelve or thirteen pizzas and several cases of sodas and I'd found the latest bootleg movies for those who had to wait out a game or simply grew tired of playing. All in all the kids had a ball and went off on their Thanksgiving breaks happy with what I hoped to be a fondness when it came to thoughts of returning to school.

I sincerely believe that school should foster a love for learning amongst our children and not the drudgery it has become in great deal due to our teachers who simply lack the creativity to inspire others and have no clue to as to what teaching requires or is all about. For most that I have witnessed who proclaim themselves teachers teaching is no more than a viable means of paying the bills—nothing more, nothing less and comes at the expense of our greatest natural resource our children. Teachers that stand before children with no sense or love for those before them other than to pick up a paycheck are doing a disservice to the profession.

Teaching is perhaps one of the most demanding professions known to man. A good teacher must first look at each and every one of his students as his own child. If race, religion or ethnic backgrounds come into play as a reason to not love and accept that student as being your own child then you cannot be a teacher and should not be in the classroom.

A teacher must also have the creativity of an actor—ready to incite a crowd and evoke emotion—always keeping them back on their heels and guessing. It is a teacher's responsibility to not only keep her children focused and on task but to create a positive and exciting learning environment where students want to learn and broaden their horizons.

They must be able to recognize and appreciate maximum teaching opportunities and pounce when the time arrives and inundate their children with an overabundance of knowledge and resources which will in turn cause them to venture out on their own in search of more knowledge. That is the role and responsibilities of a true teacher. To invoke a thirst for knowledge and then feed it at every opportunity using any vehicle open and within reason to do so this is our job as teachers. Our reward is not a paycheck but the smiling face of a young child that has just taken grasp of a new concept. That is our sole reward and if it is not and we are looking for more then we must do some careful introspection as to why we wanted to become teachers in the first place.

The Thanksgiving holidays ended rather abruptly with my friend Sarah, one of the school's two guidance counselors who I depended on closely to give me some insight into my kids and their families was killed in a head on collision with a drunken driver. She was the cutest little fireball full of so much energy and I could always count on her to be my liaison between my classroom and my children's home. It clearly affected the school and my kids especially as she was an integral part of their lives. It was a sad day but the school came closer in her passing and every effort in all that we did went in dedication to her memory. We would go on to win the middle school state championship that year in football.

One of the things which gave me a leg up with my students was the fact that I was from New York which automatically made me cool. The first few weeks I knew that my students had no concept of the enormity of New York City as they bombarded me with questions.

'Mr. Brown do you know Jay Z?'

'Mr. Brown do you know Biggie?'

The only affiliation they had with New York City was what came across the silver screen and I often times had mixed emotions when it came to television having had such a monumental affect on my kids. BET the largest and only Black network at the time was bringing the hottest new music videos which portrayed too many of our young Black men as thugs and gangstas. If you are somehow intent on diminishing the impact of BET on young Black teens at this time in our history consider the vehicle by which the Hip Hop culture exploded upon the scene. Hip hop fashion took over fashion for both Black and white youth and was brought to places from Tupelo, Mississippi to back roads country towns such as Raeford, North Carolina.

Now instead of the imperative being for an education which was up until this point the saving grace for the Negro race we became disconnected and looked at the one or two giants of hip hop to supply the answer to upward mobility for the race. Now every young Black man with a pen and a piece of paper was going to be the next hip hop mogul or a the next Michael Jordan.

I used to tell my boys that it was nice to dream but always have a contingency or alternative plan in case your dreams are deferred. I suggested education because that's all I know that the masses can take part in and be relatively successful at.

The National Basketball Association which only employs two hundred of the greatest basketball players in the world is quite the long shot an and unreal proposition to the millions of African American males practicing long hours each day hoping to make the cut. In the case of the music industry the odds are far greater with only three or four rappers hitting the pinnacle of success despite the millions hoping to emulate their wealth and success. And yet the media and television to be more exact sets these two options in motion as if they are real and viable options to the masses of African American males.

Now I don't expect for the media which is in the business of making money to have the interests of Black boys as their primary motivation or to investigate the results of their programming and their effects on our children. No, their motivation is to incur financial gains at any cost. And if not for the government stepping in to stop the selling of cigarettes because of the health risks involved Madison Avenue would still be promoting carcinogens so why do or should we expect them to take some special interest in our children's lives? We should not although it would be ideal if they took some responsibility for the messages they portray to our young people. Being that this is a rather superfluous thought in lieu of the reality and the reality is that the media makes billions literally off the mis-education and mis-direction of our children.

Instead of promoting the continual evolution of the intellectual, critical thinking African American male they have chosen to promote and glorify the hoodlum segment and their Horatio Algier ascent to wealth and fame. I can remember being in my mid twenties when the movie Scarface first came out and I watched as my Black brothers bought into the movie as if it were just another career venture. And I watched as stable African American communities, families and hundreds of thousands of people of color were literally destroyed by this blight. The entire complexion of New York changed with the inception of Scarface and cocaine being viewed now as a seemingly viable way out of the ghetto. The results were horrific despite the movie being a box office success. Not long after—somewhere around 1986—when the crack epidemic had taken affect I listened to two young drug dealers talking in the park one day.

'If you can't make a thousand dollars a night you're not doing something right.'

The young brother's street name was Black and I never saw Black again. I don't think Black was bragging when he made this testament. I think a young man on the grind could have easily made a thousand dollars a night. But the one thing Black didn't mention was the fact that that thousand dollars a night would amount to change when you divided that thousand dollars a night into the time spent in lock up for the distribution and intent to sell. Never was there any thought to the eventual repercussions of entering the drug trade and yet the hip hop culture and many Black males in poverty stricken urban areas embraced the movie as a way out.

I understood the glamorous allure the movie portrayed but there were now too many suffering at the hands of this new get rich quick scheme. I saw the continuous progression from the streets to incarceration and the lives of too many young Black males ruined. I watched as we let the media define us. I watched as money became the means to the ends by any means necessary. The need for material things now paramount our young boys began to emulate the material success of the rappers and gangsters they now saw on the silver screen. And cocaine was the means, the avenue to fame, success and material wealth. Too many of our young Black males lacking the parental guidance needed got caught up in this and threw their lives away behind lengthy prison sentences and jail records which will not allow them to secure gainful employment.

I blame the educational system for failure to incite our children to learn. I blame the parents for warehousing children as opposed to parenting. I do not believe I know or can explain the differences between yesteryear when I was a child and now and for fear of sounding like a Republican am certainly not wishing for those good ol' days which came complete with dogs and fire hoses. But there is a difference. And that is not to say that there are not a good number of Black families that are intact and are quite adept at raising strong, active aware young Black men and women. There are but if we lose one child because of our own negligence then that is one too many and one that we cannot afford to sacrifice if we are to continue the upliftment of the Negro.

It is our responsibility to be aware of the pitfalls that are systematic and continue to discriminate and make them known to our children. It is important to spend quality time and in that time to teach as well as learn and guide him through moral and ethical dilemmas and in so doing we help shape our children into the type of human being we would like for them to be.

When I was growing up we never had a firearm of any kind in the house. Guns to my parents were used for one thing only and that was to take a life. It didn't matter what type of life. All life was precious to them and so and because I was their son life also became precious to me. And I have never owned or had a firearm in my home. My kids feel similarly towards firearms. This is a learned behavior passed on or taught to us by our parents.

Concomitantly, we must address all the issues which we are privy to and especially those that concern us and especially with the genocide of the Black male. We owe it to our sons and daughters to educate them on how to best circumvent the potholes and navigate the storm of racism which we are confronted with each and every day.

This should be one of our first priorities and should be taught along with if not prior to the three R's so that our children are not caught by surprise and with their pants down unaware of the consequences of being unaware. Often the violence and death we incur is unavoidable but far too many of us meet our demise because we have not been schooled and educated in our own survival.

In any case, and before I stray too far from the point I contend that the media plays an inordinate role in helping to define and stereotype our young Black males and too often where there is no parental guidance aside from providing the child with the basic needs the child grows to for lack of a better word to be a feral child.

I don't know how many single Black mothers—educated Black women—whose sons have no idea who Frederick Douglass, Thurgood Marshall or Nat Turner is. And even if we are so naïve as to believe that the same man who enslaved us and forbid any type of formal education for us as a people is now suddenly concerned with our education we still have a responsibility to educate our children. In slavery the slave society knew that with the ability to think we would be a threat but ignorant we would remain docile, dependent, accepting and continue to do their bidding.

We have once again given him the reigns to our minds, and our education with the hopes that he has our welfare and best interest at heart. Some of you may see some folly with this as our African American children fall further and further behind. But it is not in the best interest of our children to criticize the powers that be when it comes to our children's education but our job to pick up the baton and finish the race. It is not the schools job to educate our children but let the schools if they are capable reinforce what we have already taught and instilled in our children at home. Far too many of us, and I mean Black people), have become too lax and apathetic when it comes to our children's education and survival.

Following the holiday break I had to reacquaint myself with my students. I listened as they rehashed the special events that made their Thanksgiving holiday special. And after listening to them I became increasingly aware of what interested them and what their lifelong goals were. Most wanted to become rappers or sports icons. Obama was not yet in office and I wondered if his being in the White House would have changed their perspective. I remained optimistic but doubtful. Politics was an avenue to for change and yet, (and I generalize), these people, my people, poor people, African Americans who were most in need of political activism had long since lost faith in a country that had long since disenfranchised them. Many were discontented, discouraged, and disinterested in a system that had failed them.

On their return to school I also received a visit from Weezus grandfather who was as warm and congenial as his wife. He brought me a shopping bag full of collard greens in appreciation for my work with his grandson who it was obvious that he loved dearly. And though I had seen a hundred and eighty degree turn in Weezus he still had a long way to go. He did his best to emulate the thugs ad hoodlums trying to procure a bad boy reputation which didn't jibe with my hopes for his forward progression.

What my boys didn't realize was that in more cases than not those they were trying to emulate did what they had to do in the name of survival. In relation to the living conditions and quality of life in the South Bronx Weezus and his classmates had the life of Reilly. Now that is not to say that all the young miscreants roaming the streets of New York were in survival mode and the crimes which they committed were therefore acceptable but from my perspective coming from a loving family such as Weezus and

Davika's there was no need to go for 'bad'. And yet they did emulating the rappers who spoke of expensive jewelry, fine women, money and cars. The gun was the vehicle by which all of these things were attainable and for some reason, (which to this day I still do not understand), my kids bought into this. And Weezus more so than anyone else.

Weezus stood no more than five feet tall and weighed no more than a hundred pounds dripping wet. And I wondered if this had anything to do with his need to be bigger and badder than those twice his size. I had similar issues growing up and so I understood the Napoleonic Complex he shouldered. I also knew that if he didn't control his need to overcompensate for his diminutive stature it would be the end of him. This idea of machismo so prominent in our young Black males consisted of brazen, braggadocio and not tempered could eventually lead to their demise. The fact that he had to be harder and tougher than those who stood heads and shoulders above him was a scary thought. I knew that this tough act would one day get him into trouble and since he was the leader of my class and everything began and ended with him I thought it best that I corral him before it was too late. The others would then fall in line. And if he somehow came to understand it just might save his life.

It was fast approaching the Christmas holidays and I had already planned to take my family and meet my parents at my sister's house in New York. From there my wife and I would fly down to the Bahamas for New Years. My parents would bring my kids back to North Carolina and care for them while I was away.

At school my kids were beginning to grow restless in anticipation of the long break and so I made them a proposition. With Valeria, Mr. James and I acting as judges we would decide who was the Student-of-the-Month. And to the winner I promised a Christmas with Mr. Brown and his family in New York. They were ecstatic and I had a plan.

Out of all my students Weezus was by far my brightest and had the best chance of winning if he could control his behavior. His behavior up until now had been exemplary but I always sat on the edge of my chair wondering what would be the trigger that would set him off or if someone would question his toughness and force him to reassert himself and his reputation as a tough guy.

Stopping by to talk to his grandmother one day she commended me on the contest.

'That's all Weezus talks about. I think he already has his suitcase packed.'

I smiled at the thought.

'Well, he's got some pretty stiff competition but between you and me I hope he does win. He certainly has the capabilities and his test grades, homework and class participation are excellent. And if his behavior remains the way it is he should be a shoo-in.'

'You know his grandfather and I were just telling Weezus at dinner just the other night how blessed he is to have a teacher like Mr. Brown. And even if he doesn't win those kids as well as Mr. Langdon should be thankful to have a teacher who is willing to give up his Christmas holidays to take his students with him on vacation to New York. You know a lot of these kids have never left Raeford. I want you to know it's a wonderful thing you're doing.'

What she didn't know was that I loved those kids and to have them in my company aside from the rigorous tenets of the classroom was as much of a blessing to me as any there was to have. In the following weeks Weezus took on some other additional responsibilities. Months ago thought to be the worst miscreant since John Dillinger claimed the moniker Public Enemy Number One Weezus' whole demeanor underwent a transformation of significant proportions.

Now fluent in the art of positive manipulation I sent him here and there to do my bidding. If I needed a rush order on some worksheets I sent him to the office to woo the secretary working and in minutes he was back with a large grin and the worksheets. Now instead of butting heads he matched wit with charm and watched it work for him. He was getting quite proficient in his new role and more often than not someone would stop me and comment on Weezus' behavior. He was coming around nicely and yet deep down inside of him and no matter how much we talked about it there was still that element that called to him from the underworld. I tried to steer him to some of his rap idols for the same lesson I was telling him but Scarface and BET had long before convinced him that success came with Dom Perignon, fancy cars and lots of jewelry.

As was predicted Weezus won the Student-of-the-Month Award hands down with his closest competitor light years behind. We were to board Amtrak the following day and I took Weezus home with me that night so as not to have to double back in the morning. He and my son Chris played a basketball video game for half the night and I did not interfere hoping that they'd sleep the eight hours on the train.

Once on the train I took Chris and Weezus on a mini tour showing them the bathrooms and lounge car where they could grab a snack and stretch their legs. Back in our seats Weezus occupied himself by listening to music and playing a handheld video game after talking to half the passengers on the train. But after a couple of hours and with Chris now sleep Weezus grew bored.

'Mr. Brown is it alright if I go up to the lounge car for awhile.'

I saw no reason why he couldn't and with my permission he was off but after about an hour I grew concerned and decided to see what was so enticing and had captured his attention for this long. Entering the lounge car I was surprised to find Weezus sitting with three middle aged white men in suits and ties.

'Everything okay?' I said eyeing them wearily .

'Everything's fine. Just hope you'll give our little friend Weezus here time to win some of our money back.'

I looked at Weezus and could see every one of his thirty two pearly teeth grinning at me.

'You okay?' I said now turning my attention to Weezus.

'I'm fine,' he said still grinning at me.

'You just oughta be kid. You've taken all my travel money,' the eldest of the three gentlemen commented. Seeing that the three men meant no harm I returned to my seat. Weezus arrived about an hour later the smile now permanently etched upon his face.

'How did you do?'

'I'm up about a hundred and twenty dollars and the only reason it's not more is because they got off at the last stop.'

'How much did you start off with?'

"Twelve dollars.'

'I'd say that's a pretty fair days work.'

Weezus smiled not knowing that that was forty dollars more than I made a day teaching.

We finally arrived in New York and made our way outside of Grand Central to breathe in some of that refreshing New York air. It had been years since I'd been home and it felt good to return. Weezus was overwhelmed by the sheer enormity of it all staring up at the skyscrapers which surrounded us.

'Don't stare at the buildings Weezus. That's the first indication that you're a tourist and that's like setting yourself up. A person sees that and you've identified yourself as a mark,' my wife, a native New Yorker herself, whispered to Weezus who quickly dropped his gaze.

The thirteen year old was awestruck and for the first time since I'd come to know him he was speechless. New York often has that affect on out-of-towners. My cousins used to come from just outside of Pittsburgh in southwestern Pennsylvania to spend the summers with me and act in much the same manner.

We grabbed the E train out to the island where my sister was supposed to meet us and Weezus was even more amazed by the subway and the people on it.

'Don't stare at people Weezus. New Yorkers don't go for that,' my wife said to Weezus. They had a fairly good relationship and when Weezus would catch an attitude she wouldn't back down but would instead threaten him with a good butt whooping and chase him until the boy was in tears. And when she wasn't threatening him or teasing him he was on her calling her affectionately 'mom dukes' and teasing her. He respected her and now he listened intently to her instructions with the hopes that he would make it through all the fabled horror stories of New York alive.

We celebrated Christmas with my sister and her husband, played games, ate and drank perhaps a bit too much but enjoyed ourselves the way only family can do during the holidays. During the days I'd take Weezus sightseeing and he was absolutely mesmerized by all that New York had to offer. My father fell in love with the boy and together we took him to the World Trade Center, Macy's on 34th Street, Madison Square Garden, Central Park, Times Square and a host of other well known landmarks. But I knew that wasn't really what Weezus wanted to see and so my brother-in-law who grew up in Los Angeles and laughs now when he tells stories of how he used to run through gang territories on his way to and from school each day invited him up to the Army recruiting station where he worked. This was only after talking to Weezus for what seemed like hours explaining to Weezus that what he saw on television was only a glamorized facsimile to the reality of day-to-day life in the streets of any major city.

'You think the streets are cool because of what you see on television. I see people out here every day cutting and shooting each other over a couple of dollars. That shit ain't cool. You may think it is 'til that shit hits home and then that shit becomes real. I'm telling you that this shit out here is for real. I'm tellin' you it ain't no joke and it ain't cool.'

And so the following day the women went downtown shopping while we lounged around the house until it was time to go and meet my brother-in-law who worked in what was now the Dominican section of the Bronx up around 172nd Street. We arrived at a little after five and Jose was packing it up.

It's a funny thing about New York but each neighborhood has its own distinct flavor. In the summertime you can tell from the sweet aromas and music coming from the storefronts just what ethnic group lives there. And the Dominicans like all the other groups that have made the city their home have their own certain distinct flavor. Between the sweet smells of arroz con pollo to the music you can almost taste the Dominican heritage. But with all ethnic groups there is always an under culture of crime and illicit doings and the Dominicans have been swept up like countless other ethnic groups in the very profitable drug trade. And in some parts of the Bronx the drug game has produced boundaries on streets where there were no boundaries and an incursion into someone else's territory can all too often play out in the streets. This is not what I wanted to take place but it was important to know where you were and the dangers that came with the territory. Jose and I had given Weezus the rundown and at last elicited some fear in the teenager. My father who had accompanied us earlier went on up to Jose's office. But being that it was coming close to our final days in the city and Weezus still wanted to pick up a couple of things to take back I took him down to Canal Street where he'd be able to shop on the street and save a few dollars.

Coming up the subway stairs in the Bronx around the corner from Jose's office two boys eased up against a boy coming up the stairs and accosted him for his gold chain. Weezus was shocked and chose to stop and stare but I pushed him along quickly as if nothing happened. New Yorkers do not get involved in other's affairs unless the odds are clearly in their favor. And me alone with someone else's child was not about to play Good Samaritan against two toughs who were bad enough to stop someone coming up the stairs and force him to remove his jewelry and give it to them or suffer the consequences. Weezus had never witnessed a robbery and was quite shaken by the whole affair and began to relate it to my father and brother-in-law when Jose stopped him.

'I don't want to hear about it. I told you I see it every day. I told you that shit ain't cool. I just pray that one day it won't be me. 'Cause anyone that tries to stick me up for my gold or my money is a dead man. They'll have to kill me first.'

Weezus did't say a word and the next minute we were back in the cold December air walking briskly toward the subway. It was dark and the streets were all but empty now. Towards the middle of the block a small crowd of about five or six young toughs stood in front of a now closed storefront. Weezus was holding one hand and Chris my other as we neared the young men standing. I knew that the only people braving this cold were those making their money plying their craft and continued walking when Weezus pulled my hand trying to get me to cross the street.

My father noticed the boy's fear and calmly said, 'Walk straight ahead Weezus.' We did so and once amongst the young men my father said 'Evening fellas.' At which time they grunted and nodded as we passed through.

When we returned to school following the Christmas break everyone was chomping at the bit to hear all about Weezus' trip to the big city. I was also interested to hear his rendition. And when he finished I knew two things had taken place. New York by its sheer magnitude and enormity had had the profound effect of finally placing everything in proper perspective. There was a much larger world out there than he could have ever dreamed and that world was so sprawling and wild that he would not could not have possibly survived. He now had perspective.

The other thing I heard when he recounted the story of the robbery was how messed up it was that this poor kid who hadn't done nothin' got jacked for his chain. So, after all the rap and talk of taking whatever it was we wanted the actual event unfolding before his eyes brought quite a different response. And the perceived possibility of violence a few minutes later refuted every rap myth about the storied glamour of violence and street life. The reality was quite different and there was no classroom, nor curriculum that could have provided a more thorough and pervasive lesson than this week in New York City.

I liked the fact that Weezus was brash, hungry and proud. There was nothing unusual about a teenage boy feeling invincible as he came closer to manhood but in lieu of the pending odds and response to this behavior it had to be tempered and used in a positive manner. That is if he is to make a serious stab at manhood in our society. I think the visit to New York City had that type of calming effect on the boy.

My father who by this time had become very fond of Weezus commented that Weezus was a bright, kid and was more of a challenge for the educational system than the slower child at the other end of the intellectual spectrum. For a bright child was inquisitive and because he was quick to pick up concepts he bored easily and often times became disruptive.

This was the case when we speak of Weezus and because of a limited class size and the recognition that he was bright and his spirit acknowledged as being that of a thirteen year old full of vim and vigor as he entered puberty we understood embraced his vitality and had no problem other than how to best guide him into manhood.

Six or seven years later my mother was shopping at the local Wal-Mart when she ran into Weezus grandmother who stopped her.

'Ms. Brown it is so good to see you. How's your son?'

'He's doing fine. How's Weezus and your family?'

'Doing beautifully… Weezus is a sophomore at the University of Tennessee. He made the dean's list last semester.'

CPSIA information can be obtained
at www.ICGtesting.com
Printed in the USA
LVOW13s2030130917
548620LV00014B/188/P